BREAKING FREE

EXPOSING the NATURE of ADDICTION

Addiction thrives in darkness.

And guess what? That means we need to

turn on the light! Many are afraid to flip that switch

because of the painful truths that will be exposed.

But the light of truth is the only way

to clearly see our path forward.

Will you flip that switch?

By: Wendy Buttacy

Breaking Free: Exposing The Nature of Addiction

By: Wendy Buttacy M.A.

Design: Peggy Niebuhr

ISBN: 978-1-944933-58-6

This study is designed for use by Adult & Teen Challenge USA as a part of their Personal Studies for New Life in Christ (PSNL) curriculum; developed for those interested in spiritual growth. The PSNL are designed for use in an individualized educational program. This PSNL study must be purchased through Adult & Teen Challenge USA. For more information contact:

Adult & Teen Challenge USA
Phone: 417-581-2181
E-mail: tcusa@teenchallengeusa.org
Website: https://teenchallengeusa.org

Adult & Teen Challenge

PSNL: GOALS & STRUCTURE

Each Personal Study for New Life in Christ (PSNL) is designed to be completed in one week (one chapter per day) and should take roughly 30-45 min. per day to complete. We recommend that you don't do more than one chapter per day, as each has specific prayer and application points to focus on. This will give you time to process the information and to think about how to apply it to your life.

These studies are designed to challenge us in different ways. They cause us to evaluate our beliefs, behaviors, feelings, & habits regarding the topic covered. More importantly, they challenge us to filter our lives through a Biblical world view: "What does God have to say about all of this?"

To better develop this Biblical filter, we will open each study with a Core Scripture, Challenge Points, & Sticky Points sections and end with Growth Points. Before you start your chapter for the day, take time to read your Core Scripture for the week and work through your Challenge Points. When you complete the study, you can summarize it all by completing your Growth Points.

CORE SCRIPTURE OF THE WEEK ———

Each PSNL study opens with a CORE SCRIPTURE. This Scripture is central to the topic being covered in each study, and we highly recommend that you commit the Core Scripture to memory. Psalms 119 says that the Word of God is a LIGHT and a LAMP, showing us the way in which to go. Investing in memorizing God's Word never comes back void. It provides us with a road map for life.

WHAT ARE CHALLENGE POINTS? ———

The word "challenge" is important because challenges are often catalysts for change and growth. The Bible tells us that: "the Word of God is ALIVE and ACTIVE. Sharper than any double-edged sword, it penetrates even to dividing soul and spirit, joints and marrow; it judges the THOUGHTS and ATTITUDES of the HEART" (Hebrews 4:12).

If God's word is alive and active, we should treat it that way. We must put it into practice. By focusing each week on new Challenge Points, we are investing in this truth by putting His Word into practice and allowing the Lord to challenge the thoughts and attitudes of our hearts.

Psalms 34:8 encourages us to, "TASTE and SEE that the Lord is good." Challenge points are a way for us to "taste and see" that God is good and that His Word is active and alive. Even if you are struggling with your faith or haven't committed to a relationship with Christ, we encourage you to "taste and see" that GOD is GOOD. Try out and invest in these challenge points each week and see what happens. Over time, we hope that you come to know not only His goodness and His blessings, but that you also come to know HIM.

PSNL: GOALS & STRUCTURE

 ## WHAT ARE STICKY POINTS? —————————————

Sticky Points are a way for us to reflect on what stuck with us from our previous week's PSNL work. They are thoughts, ideas, or feelings that we just can't seem to shake off. Oftentimes, these sticky points are the HOLY SPIRIT bringing important truths to our attention or they are ideas that we have trouble understanding or accepting. At other times we may experience strong feelings regarding what we are learning, and we need to take time to process and examine those feelings.

Regardless of where these Sticky Points come from, it is important to address them so we do not miss opportunities to grow or get stuck (have trouble learning/applying new truths as we move forward). If there are any Sticky Points that are bringing you to the point of distraction, we encourage you to talk to the Lord about them in prayer and to ask your facilitator/discipleship staff to help you work through them.

 ## WHAT ARE GROWTH POINTS? —————————————

You will learn new information and process a lot of thoughts/emotions as you work through these PSNL studies. So, we need to digest all of this in bite-sized pieces to ensure that it sticks with us. One way to do this is to process the material as we go. In our GROWTH POINTS section (at the end of each study), we will pose questions like: "What did I learn this week?" "How does this apply to my life?" and "What action steps can I take?"

As you answer these questions, we hope to connect the dots of how this new information fits into your day-to-day life. Learning truth is one thing, but applying it to our lives is more important because we believe that the Word of God is ACTIVE and ALIVE.

CONTENTS

This Week's Challenge

CORE SCRIPTURE

"Praise the Lord, my soul, and forget not all his benefits—who forgives all your sins and heals all your diseases, who redeems your life from the pit and crowns you with love and compassion, who satisfies your desires with good things so that your youth is renewed like the eagle's."

Psalms 103:2-5 (NIV)

CHALLENGE POINTS

READ:

The Core Scripture above 1-2 times each day this week. Want to take it up a notch? Try memorizing the Scripture along the way.

REFLECT:

Answer the following questions after you read the Core Scripture.

Try to think of new answers each day:

 How does the way you act reflect these truths—that you are forgiven, healed, redeemed, crowned, and renewed?

 How much do you think these benefits are worth?

 What would need to change for you to embrace these blessings?

PRAY:

Spend 5-10 minutes of your prayer time asking God to help you embrace His forgiveness, healing, redemption, and renewal. Ask Him to replace your desires for destructive, addictive behaviors with good things.

TASTE & SEE (Psalm 34:8):

This week take on an attitude of praise and thankfulness. Despite how you might currently feel, begin to thank God for forgiving, healing, redeeming, and renewing you. Pay attention to how your attitudes begin to change as you attune your heart to Him.

STICKY POINTS

List what you learned from last week's PSNL work that stuck with you or that you are wrestling with. Are there any ideas, thoughts, or emotions that you just can't shake? Anything that strongly impacted you (good or bad)? List them below. (If this is your first week, please disregard this section.)

WHAT IS THIS STUDY ABOUT?

You are in a spiritual battle. Whether you accept that as truth or not, it remains true. You are more than just flesh and blood or the sum of your DNA. You are made in the image of God—spirit and flesh, but born into a sinful, fallen world. And despite that sinfulness, God loves you. He gave His only son, Jesus, to free you from the darkness of sin and become your light!

But you also have an enemy—satan. He wants to kill your hope, steal your peace, and destroy your future. His currency is shame, deception, and darkness. We live in a fallen world and temptations are everywhere. So, how do we step out of that darkness and stay out? WE SHINE THE LIGHT OF TRUTH!

We no longer cower in darkness and fear. We root ourselves in light by seeking truth. This PSNL series (107-607) will expose the truth about ourselves, our sins, their consequences, and, most importantly, the power of Jesus to redeem it all. But it won't be easy. Confronting the truth is a difficult and often painful process. So, why do it? Because to do so honors Jesus' sacrifice. We honor Him by standing in our truth and surrendering it all to Him. Not just the parts we are proud of or the parts we can stomach, all of it—the good, the bad, and the ugly.

> ## What if I'm not ready for that?

You will never be fully ready. It's a step of faith. But don't worry, God is patient with us not wanting anyone to be lost in darkness. You don't have to confront it all right now. It's a journey, allowing God to shine His light in and through you. And as He does, you are transformed day by day, moment by moment. DARKNESS TURNS INTO LIGHT!

Even if you're not sure if you believe in God, I challenge you to go on a journey with us in this study to discover truth…to discover Him.

> ## Isn't this study about addiction?

For once you were darkness, but now you are light in the Lord…Have nothing to do with the fruitless deeds of darkness, but rather expose them…But everything exposed by the light becomes visible—and everything that is illuminated becomes light.

(Ephesians 5:8,11,13)

Yes, it's about exposing addiction! We will take what thrives (grows) in darkness and expose it to the light of God's Word—destroying its power. The truth is that we are all born addicted…addicted to sin. We may have different addictions (i.e. drugs, alcohol, pornography, rage, lust, sex, gossip), but we all face this truth.

The question is, will you join the battle? Will you cower in darkness, defeated, or will you go on a journey with us and step into the light? Will you fight back by seeking truth? We won't hold back any punches. We will expose the very nature of addiction and how it affects us physically, mentally, and emotionally. We will also confront the destructive path it carves into our relationships with God and others. This won't be an easy journey but hope, joy, and freedom await us on the other side. Let's expose this darkness by turning on the LIGHT!

Exposing Darkness

Our Question:

WHY DO WE NEED TO UNDERSTAND ADDICTION?

Addict. That's who I am at my core. It's in my DNA. My parents, grandparents, aunts, uncles, and even my kids are addicts. Our drug of choice may differ, but we all give in to it. Even when I'm sober, I think and talk like an addict.

I can fake it for the benefit of others, but I know the truth. I've got a terminal condition, a lifelong diagnosis.

All I can do is fight it off as best I can and stay in constant treatment. If I let my guard down for even a moment, I'm in just as deep as I was before.

Sometimes I wonder why I even try. I can't change one bit of it. If God is real, He's dealt me the worst hand in the deck. How can He judge me when He allowed me to be born this way?

~Helplessly Addicted

Sinner. That's who I am, at my core. Alcoholism is just the latest reflection of that reality. I've lied, stolen, hurt, and broken people to feed my addictions— every instance a choice. Choices I made without giving them a second thought.

People have spoken to me about redemption and God's love for me, but I know the truth. I don't deserve redemption. Forgiving me would dirty God's character. If God is good, then He would never want me. I deserve every judgement that comes my way.

To top it all off, I'm a coward. I can't even stomach the idea of approaching God and confirming the truth that I already know… that I'm irredeemable (a lost cause). All that's left is to enjoy what cheap thrills I can before the end. There is no hope for me.

~Hopelessly Addicted

FINDING MEANING

Well, this didn't start off with rainbows and sunshine, did it?!?

I did say we weren't going to hold back any punches. If we're going to expose darkness, then we need to get real, fast. These scenarios reflect two ways people define addiction—AN ILLNESS TO TREAT (not cure) or SIN. People will even debate between these two views passionately. Why? Because many of us don't have the same or even clear definitions of addiction and sin.

Here are two simple definitions for us to work with:

ADDICTION
The condition of being physically and/or mentally dependent on a substance or activity and being unable to stop without having adverse (negative) effects.

SIN
"Any thought or action that falls short (misses the mark) of God's (perfect) will." -Billy Graham

Side Note: *The condition of being addicted in and of itself isn't sin. But if you are addicted to sinful activities (behaviors that are outside of God's will) and actively choose to dwell or act on those impulses, that is sinful.*

For Example: *I could experience the effects of withdrawal from drugs or alcohol and have a strong impulse to use, but if I abstain, I am choosing to put sin to death. Or, I could be dependent on spending time with God, not want to quit, and have adverse effects if I stop. That's not a sinful dependence.*

But when we talk about addiction, we aren't talking about actions that honor God's will. We are talking about addictions to destructive behaviors (life-controlling problems) that wreak havoc on our lives and the people around us. These come in many forms, such as: gambling, drugs/alcohol, unhealthy/immoral sexual behaviors, pornography, and even video game/social media/internet addictions.

What do all of these have in common?

➤ TEMPORARY HIGHS/REWARDS

➤ GROWING TOLERANCE   must increase behaviors to get the same high/reward

➤ NEGATIVE IMPACT— spiritual, physical, mental, emotional, and/or social consequences

➤ WITHDRAWAL— negative (unpleasant) effects when we stop the behaviors

➤ IDOLATRY— dependence on a substance/activity instead of God

Why do we need to understand or define addiction?

Because if we don't, your ENEMY (satan) will. Look at these opening scenarios. Can you see the lies woven within? Two separate ways to define addiction, both twisted by lies. Satan wants you stuck in sin (separated from God), and there is no better way to do that than to keep you addicted to it. He uses TEMPTATIONS to pull us into sinful behaviors and DECEPTION to push us towards addiction.

Here are three of his most common deceptions (two are outlined in our opening scenarios):

DENIAL	HELPLESSNESS	HOPELESSNESS
"I don't have a problem."	"I have a problem, but it's a disease with no cure."	"I have a problem, but it makes me a sinner undeserving of redemption."

Can you see how believing these lies can push us further into addiction? It goes from a straight up lie (denial) to half-truths twisted into extreme lies. Is acting on an addiction to something outside of God's will sinful? Yes. Does recovery from the effects of addiction take ongoing healing/help? Yes. Addiction often has long-term effects or consequences that we must address.

But these are only half-truths. The rest of the story is that...
➤ Forgiveness is available for ALL through faith in Jesus.
➤ We can become NEW CREATIONS (fully healed and restored).
➤ ONGOING healing, direction, and freedom is available as you ACTIVELY ENGAGE in a relationship with God.
➤ Total and complete freedom is possible.
➤ "Addict" doesn't have to be your identity!

THERE IS HOPE AND YOU ARE NOT HELPLESS! To overcome these lies, we must learn the whole truth about the nature of addiction and the power of God. We must avoid tunnel vision—focusing on half-truths. These can too easily turn into false beliefs or doubt.

For Example: *A staff member at one of our Adult & Teen Challenge centers once told me his story which helped inspire this study. As a student, he came to know Jesus and to believe that he was a new creation. But he never learned about the effects/consequences of his past addiction. So, when he returned home, he was blindsided by his own struggle with temptations to use and the consequences of his past choices. He started to doubt. Was something wrong with him? Is there really freedom in Jesus? If so, why was he still struggling?*

We don't want you to be blindsided. We want to expose the full nature of addiction and how it can affect each part of your life so that you can be prepared. We want to arm you with truth and wisdom so that you can walk through tough times with strength, faith, and hope.

We also want you to know that you are not alone. If you are just starting a program or realizing that you have a problem, you may be experiencing the effects of withdrawal from that addiction. This study will help you to better understand and manage the thoughts and feelings you are walking through today.

 LET'S CHECK-IN

1. How have you viewed or defined addiction in the past?

   _____

   _____

2. Has your view or definition affected your behaviors positively or negatively? Why?

_____

_____

_____

3. How has denial, helplessness, or hopelessness been a struggle for you?

_____

_____

_____

TALK IT OUT

➤ *If I don't believe in God, how will this study relate to me?*

Despite your beliefs about God, truth is truth. Not only will we study the spiritual effects of addiction, but also the physical, mental, emotional, and social effects. You will be able to relate to these as we explore them in more depth each day. But I also want to challenge you: start this study with an open mind. Look at the scriptures we study and consider their substance. Ask yourself, is this truth? Would this help me? What would my life look like if I carried this out?

The first two steps of any 12-step program are to accept that you can't fix things on your own and to believe that a higher power can help. If you do this, you might be surprised by who meets you along the way. Even if you don't believe in God, I can tell you with assurance that He doesn't just believe in you—He loves you.

➤ *What's all this talk about exposing darkness?*

Life-controlling and destructive addictions thrive in DARKNESS. If you have struggled with addiction this isn't shocking. Just think about how far you've gone to hide addictive behaviors from others. Why do we do this? Because exposure is deadly to addiction. When others see we have a problem, they stop enabling it. They set boundaries that force us to either get help or get out.

But the greatest darkness is the one we surround ourselves with—*I don't have a problem.* We deny, deny, deny. We will talk about denial in more detail in PSNL 207, but we will begin to strip it of its power this week as we expose the truth about addiction.

In fact, the only way to overcome darkness is to expose it to the light—THE TRUTH. Psalms 119:105 says that the Word of God is a lamp for our feet (directing our steps) and a light on our path (showing us where to go). Today we will go to God's Word (the Bible) to reveal the true nature of addiction.

SEARCHING SCRIPTURE

> *How does addiction affect us?*

DIVERSE EFFECTS

Let's Read: **Proverbs 23:29-35** (NIV)

This passage lays out the effects of drunkenness by asking: Who has woe? Who has

_____? Who has _____? Who has complaints? Who has needless

_____? In the end, drunkenness bites like a snake and _____ like a

viper. Your eyes will see strange sights, and your _____ will imagine confusing things.

Even though this passage is talking about alcohol, these truths apply to all destructive addictions. We see here that drunkenness affects us emotionally by causing great sorrow. It affects our relationships by causing strife. It causes physical harm to our bodies (bruises, bloodshot eyes, and much worse). Addiction also deceives our minds, and Galatians 5:21 (which we will study tomorrow) teaches that addictions to sinful activities affect us spiritually by separating us from God.

Addiction is a poison that affects your entire being. Each day this week, we will focus on one of these areas: the SPIRITUAL, PHYSICAL, MENTAL, SOCIAL, AND EMOTIONAL effects of addiction. We will expose this poisonous darkness to the light—the healing power of God's truth.

> *Is there hope for overcoming these effects?*

OUR HOPE – HEALING & FORGIVENESS

Let's Read: **Psalms 103:1-5 & 2 Corinthians 5:17** (NIV)

The Psalms praise the Lord for his benefits: God forgives all our _____ and _____ all our

diseases. He _____ our lives from the pit and crowns us with love and compassion. He

satisfies our _____ with good things so that our youth is renewed like the eagle's.

2 Corinthians teaches that if anyone is in _____, the new _____ has
come: the old has gone, the new is here!

Is there hope? Absolutely! No matter how you view addiction (as an illness, sin, or a combo) the solution is the same. God HEALS our illnesses and FORGIVES our sins. JESUS is the solution no matter what label you put on it. He can satisfy your desires with good things! You can become a new creation in Christ! God can restore and renew us from the effects of addiction(s).

But this requires us to put our FAITH IN JESUS. He suffered for our healing. He died so that we can be forgiven. He rose from the grave so that we can have eternal life.

But we must confess (speak) that Jesus is Lord and believe that God raised Him from the dead. We must invite God into our lives and accept the healing, forgiveness, and life He provides. He won't force us to accept these gifts.

LET'S CHECK-IN

1. How has addiction affected you or the lives of those you know? List the first three things that come to mind.

   _____

   _____

   _____

2. Do you have hope that these effects can be overcome? If yes, where do you find your hope? If no, why?

   _____

   _____

   _____

3. Is it hard to believe that healing and forgiveness can be found through faith in Jesus? Why?

   _____

   _____

   _____

TALK IT OUT

> *So, if I don't believe in Jesus, I have no hope?!*

You still have hope for change, but it's LIMITED. Without handling the spiritual effects of addiction, recovery isn't complete. Many without faith view addiction as a lifelong condition for this very reason. They take steps to change their behaviors and treat some of the effects of addiction, but it's still a lifelong battle. They continue to identify as an addict in recovery—not a new creation.

You can grow and learn a lot about addiction from this study. However, you may not experience the level of freedom we are describing if you refuse to acknowledge the spiritual roots and effects of addiction. Complete freedom comes only through a relationship with Jesus. He meets our spiritual needs, empowering us to dig addiction up by its roots.

> *It seems like a fairy tale to believe that Jesus will cure all my problems.*

Let's be clear. We're not saying that putting faith in Jesus heals, restores, and renews every area of our lives all at once. We still walk through the consequences of our past actions. But there is an immediate, eternal salvation that occurs when we put our faith in Jesus. This restores our relationship with God here and now. We experience spiritual cleansing and forgiveness, but it doesn't end there.

That restored relationship with God opens a door that invites Him to work in our lives. There are many wounds, weaknesses, and false beliefs that need correction or healing. Some wounds receive immediate healing, others heal over time. As we build our relationship with God, we learn to listen and follow His voice. He then leads us into increased healing, freedom, and transformation.

So, faith in Jesus gives us hope for IMMEDIATE and ONGOING healing. It isn't some fairy tale separate from reality. We still walk through hardship, pain, and temptation, but we no longer walk alone. Jesus leads the way.

 # WHAT HAVE WE LEARNED?

> *Our Question: Why do we need to understand addiction?*

Two common ways people view addiction: an illness to treat (not cure) or _____.

The condition of being physically and/or mentally dependent on a substance or activity and being unable to stop without adverse effects is _____.

Any thought or action that falls short (misses the mark) of God's perfect will is: _____.

If we don't understand and define addiction, our _____ (satan) will. He uses _____ to push us towards addiction.

The three most common deceptions are denial, _____, and hopelessness.

The truth is that forgiveness is available to _____ through faith in Jesus and we can become new _____ (with hope for healing and restoration).

Life-controlling and destructive addictions thrive in _____. The only way to overcome this darkness is to expose it to the light—the truth.

Addiction is a poison that has spiritual, physical, _____, social, and emotional effects.

But there is hope because God _____ our illnesses and _____ our sins.

This hope requires us to put our faith in _____ for immediate and _____ healing.

ACTION PLAN

1 If you are struggling with feelings of helplessness or hopelessness, it's important to acknowledge those feelings and to identify where they come from. Complete the following statements below as they apply to you.

I sometimes feel helpless because:

_____

_____

_____

I sometimes feel hopeless because:

_____

_____

_____

When I think about putting faith in Jesus I feel: _____

Why?

_____

_____

_____

2 Write down your thoughts or a prayer about what it would take for you to put your faith fully in Jesus. Be honest about your thoughts, hopes, doubts, and fears.

_____

_____

_____

_____

_____

_____

_____

_____

_____

_____

Discuss your thoughts or questions about this chapter with your facilitator. Have them check your work and sign here before starting the next chapter.

Facilitator's Signature: _____

Shiny Objects

WHAT DOES THE BIBLE SAY ABOUT ADDICTION?

Empty. That's the only way to describe it. I was empty. No matter what I filled myself with, it always sifted through. Nothing stuck, nothing satisfied, and nothing filled the gaping holes I felt beneath the surface.

It was not for lack of effort. I committed everything...lost everything...to fill the void. I wanted to feel everything and anything—just not empty. I gravitated toward anything shiny.

Drugs, alcohol, and sex were my favorite shiny objects. They appealed to my pride. I wanted to feel like a god. But really, I wanted to be anything other than me—to step out of myself and my life. I wanted something I couldn't name and couldn't reach.

But the further I reached, the larger the holes stretched. What appeared shiny, proved poisonous—corroding the pieces that were still intact. It all sifted through even faster. I had to do and sacrifice more to feel anything at all.

I could feel myself begin to slip through the cracks, my identity ripped away. In the end, all that was left was a new identity—addict. This was my reality, helpless and hopeless, until—I gave up.

I stopped reaching, trying to fill the holes on my own. I admitted defeat and gave in to the emptiness...the stillness...the quiet.

In that place of despair, I heard a small voice repeat a phrase I had heard long ago, "Be still and know that I am God" (Psalm 46:10). It was a sliver of light that I chose to ignore—turning away in shame and anger.

But the voice persisted. "I am the light of the world." *That's great*, I thought, *but I'm in darkness*. "Whoever follows me will never walk in darkness but will have the light of life" (John 8:12). That made me pause. The "light of life" was something foreign, new.

Show me this light! I thought. And He opened my eyes. It was as if a burst of light struck my soul. I had been blind—walking in darkness with my eyes closed to the truth.

I was made in the image of God. Fallen and sinful, but still His. This was the void I felt. My emptiness was a lack of His presence. And as I surrendered my life into His hands, I felt full... satisfied...complete. My old identity slipped away because it had never been complete. I was a child of God—a child of light!

~Searching for Identity

◉ FINDING MEANING

This is where we talk about the God-shaped hole in my heart, right?

Well, if you want to sound cliché…sure. But it's more about your design and structure. Mankind is the only species made in the IMAGE OF GOD (Gen. 1:27). We are unique—set apart. Designed to live in relationship with God, and to care for, protect, and rule the created world (Gen. 1:28-30).

That design includes the capacity for the Holy Spirit of God to dwell (live) within us (1 Cor. 6:19). We are made of flesh but also SPIRIT. The fruit (benefits) of God's Spirit are love, joy, peace, patience, kindness, goodness, faithfulness, gentleness, and self-control (Gal. 5:22-23). Without God, we struggle to experience and live out these qualities.

We are designed to run on an everlasting, high voltage power supply (God's Spirit) but are born running on AA batteries (our flesh). We have a deep desire to feel love, joy, and peace, but we fall short. This leaves a VOID. We burn through weak power supplies faster and faster, trying to fulfill a purpose we can't put our finger on. It's maddening. Some of us will try anything that gives us temporary highs or smooth lows—SHINY OBJECTS.

One of my favorite sayings is, *not everything that glimmers is gold*. In fact, the shiny objects of life (the fast highs or easy roads) are always fake—fool's gold.

How does this apply to addiction?

Addiction is something we fall into when we chase shiny objects (temporary highs). We try to fill a spiritual void with a COUNTERFEIT (fool's gold). If you want to understand the nature of addiction, we must first understand something about ourselves. We must acknowledge that we are flesh and spirit. Today, we will look at how addictions affect us spiritually. But to do so, we must first understand our original spiritual condition.

What is our original spiritual condition?

Our spiritual condition upon birth, is SINFUL (Romans 3:23), and we are born into a fallen world. One could even say that we are born in WITHDRAWAL, separated from God's presence by sin. We are desperate to fill this void as we grow and mature. And if we turn our eyes to shiny objects, we can become addicted to sinful, destructive behaviors that never truly satisfy.

Can you see why understanding this spiritual condition is important? If we don't recognize the true problem, our only hope relies on plugging in AA's (counterfeits) to keep us running at fifty percent. We must first acknowledge that we have a SPIRITUAL NEED. A need that can only be satisfied through a RELATIONSHIP WITH GOD. We need to plug-in to His Spirit.

✓ LET'S CHECK-IN

1. Have you ever felt an emptiness or spiritual void? What was this like for you?

   _____

   _____

   _____

2. What are your shiny objects? What have you used to fill feelings of emptiness?

   _____

   _____

   _____

3. What thoughts or feelings do you have about God being the solution to the emptiness you have felt?

   _____

   _____

   _____

📖 SEARCHING SCRIPTURE

> *What if I don't buy into this spiritual stuff?*

Again, what do you have to lose by considering it? If you are right, you have nothing to lose. If you are wrong, you have everything to gain. The wise choice is to not rule anything out. Investigate the spiritual effects of addiction with us today with an open mind.

> *What does the Bible say about the spiritual nature of addiction?*

A DARK NATURE

Let's Read: **Galatians 5:19-21 & 1 Corinthians 10:6-7;14** (NIV)

Galatians teaches that the acts of the flesh are sexual immorality, impurity and _____; idolatry and witchcraft; hatred, discord, jealousy, fits of rage, selfish ambition, dissensions, factions and envy; _____, and orgies. Those who live like this will not inherit the kingdom of

_____.

1 Corinthians tells us to keep from setting our hearts on _____ things and to not be

_____. In fact, verse 14 says we should _____ from idolatry.

Destructive, life-controlling addictions involve ACTS OF THE FLESH. Acts of the flesh are sinful behaviors (behaviors that are outside of God's will for us). And God's will is to see us whole, healthy, and in relationship with Him. He wants to bless us. Following God's will is not a punishment, but a joy.

In contrast, acts of the flesh are destructive and addictive. The definition of *debauchery* (one of the acts of the flesh listed above) is too much use or participation in sensual pleasures. Most addictions fit this description.

Addiction is also a form of IDOLATRY. Idolatry is the practice of worshipping and following an idol. An idol is anything we setup as a god in our lives; we worship it and bow down to it. We let it dictate what we do. Our desires for these idols take center stage instead of God's will for our lives. Does this sound familiar? Addiction, by its definition, becomes idolatry.

> *What are the spiritual consequences of addiction?*

SPIRITUAL CONSEQUENCES

Let's Read: **Galatians 6:8**, **Ephesians 5:5 & Jonah 2:8** (NIV)

Galatians teaches that those who work to please their _____ will reap (receive)

_____, but those who work to please the Spirit will reap (receive) eternal life.

The passage in Jonah describes idolatry as turning away from God's _____ for us.

Ephesians teaches us that no idolater will inherit the kingdom of _____ and of _____.

When we look at the spiritual effects (consequences) of sin, we realize just how much we have to lose in this battle. These spiritual consequences are both immediate and eternal. Acts of the flesh cause us to reap DESTRUCTION (physically, mentally, socially, and emotionally) as those addictions cause damage in the here and now.

We are also immediately and eternally harmed by the idolatry of addiction because we "turn away from God's love for us." Our relationship with God is damaged and broken by sin. We miss out on the fruit of His Spirit (presence) in our lives which includes: love, joy, peace, patience, kindness, goodness, faithfulness, gentleness, and self-control. And if we refuse to put our faith in the grace and forgiveness offered to us through Jesus, we won't inherit eternal life. Instead, we'd face ETERNAL SEPARATION.

> *How can we overcome these spiritual consequences?*

BREAK FREE: REPENT, RETURN & RELY

STEP ONE: REPENT – Let's Read: **Ezekiel 14:1-6** (NIV)

Ezekiel tells us the story of how the Israelites had set up _____ in their hearts. But God had a plan to recapture their _____. He told them to _____ and turn from their idols.

If we want to bridge the gap between God and us, we must confess our sins and turn away from acts of the flesh and the idolatry of addiction. God will not share our devotion and worship. How powerful and humbling is it to know that God desires to recapture your whole heart? He cares for you and has meaningful plans and purposes for your life.

We must choose who we will serve. Repentance requires us to confess and turn away from sin, putting our faith in Jesus to save, redeem, and restore our relationship with God. But then what?

STEP TWO: RETURN – Let's Read: **1 Samuel 7:2-3** (NIV)

The passage in 1 Samuel shares how (at another time) Samuel told the Israelites that if they were returning to the Lord with all of their _____, they should get rid of their foreign _____ (idols), commit themselves to the Lord, and _____ Him only.

We must return to the Lord with ALL our heart. This means we get rid of anything that has to do with addiction(s) (i.e. drugs, alcohol, paraphernalia, unhealthy relationships, pornography, etc.). We need to rid our lives of anything that has become an idol.

We do this with a heart committed to loving and obeying God (instead of our own desires). We must return and serve. We serve God by choosing actions that honor Him and reflect His love. Standing idle will only lead us back into temptation. We must find a new purpose and mission by serving God.

STEP THREE: RELY– Let's Read: **Titus 2:11-12** (NIV)

Titus teaches us that the grace of God offers _____ to all people. Grace then teaches us to say "_____" to ungodliness and worldly passions, and to live self-_____, upright and godly lives.

We must learn to rely and trust in the grace of God to save and restore us. As we develop our relationship with God, the Holy Spirit empowers us to say "no" to sinful behaviors. We grow in self-control. We are changed.

A relationship with our creator is powerful. We are transformed into God's image more each day! (We will talk more about this transformation in detail in PSNL 207-607.)

Side Note: *Remember that this is a process. Grace* TEACHES *us, and this takes* TIME AND EXPERIENCE. *We must be students, willing to learn and eager to turn to the Lord when we mess up/ fall short. We must look to Him more than ourselves. When we are relying on God, mistakes become opportunities for His grace to teach and transform us.*

# LET'S CHECK-IN

1. How has addiction spiritually affected you or someone you know?

_____

_____

_____

2. What makes it difficult for you to consider repenting and/or returning to God with your whole heart?

_____

_____

_____

3. What behaviors, people, or things are difficult for you to turn away from?

_____

_____

_____

# TALK IT OUT

> *What if I don't want to repent or return to God?*

Well, as we learned from Galatians 6:8, if we sow (invest in) our own desires, we will reap destruction. But those who sow to the Spirit will reap eternal life. You can continue to ignore God, but He is patient, not wanting anyone to perish (2 Peter 3:9). He also honors your choice. He doesn't force us into repentance. Salvation is a gift that must be accepted. Just remember that He is also just; we will be held responsible for our choices and actions. I pray that you would consider accepting the gift of grace.

> *What if I've repented and turned to God but I'm still struggling to give up addictive behaviors?*

Continue to rely on and trust in God and seek help from other believers. There is no promise that this will be easy. In fact, it may be the most difficult thing you ever do. Be patient with the process. The transformation that God's grace supplies is often a MARATHON not a SPRINT.

Remember the amount of time you dedicated to your addictive behaviors in the past? Your body, mind, emotions, and relationships were hijacked by those addictive behaviors. It may take time to heal from the damage that caused.

Faith in Jesus is the starting line (ensuring your eternal salvation). While it may be tempting to call a taxi to get you to the finish line, that wouldn't allow you to win the race. You would miss the growth and lessons learned along the way. It's much wiser to remain patient, stick it out, and trust in God.

 # WHAT HAVE WE LEARNED?

> *Our Question: What does the Bible say about addiction?*

We are the only species made in the image of _____. We are flesh but also

_____.

When we chase after shiny objects (addictive behaviors) we are trying to fill a spiritual void (need)

with a _____ (fool's gold).

Our original spiritual condition upon birth is _____. We are in

_____ separated from God's presence by sin.

If we want to overcome addiction, we must first acknowledge that we have a spiritual _____

that can only be met through a relationship with _____.

Life-controlling, destructive addictions include acts of the _____ and

_____.

Acts of the flesh cause us to reap _____ and the idolatry of addiction can cause

eternal _____ from God (if we don't repent).

We can overcome these spiritual consequences if we _____ from our sins,

_____ to the Lord with all our heart, and learn to _____ on His grace.

ACTION PLAN

1 Take a few moments to think about the process of repenting, returning, and relying on God. What would this look like for you? Fill in your answers below to help you think it through.

I need to repent of the following behaviors:

_____

_____

_____

_____

2 If I return or turn to God with ALL my heart, I need to turn away from or get rid of:

_____

_____

_____

_____

_____

_____

3 Relying on and trusting in God is not easy for many of us. What makes this difficult for you? Are there wounds that need healing? Do you have doubts? Do you need to let go of pride or fear? List your answer(s) below. Bring this issue(s) to God in prayer and/or talk to someone you trust about it.

_____

_____

_____

_____

_____

_____

_____

_____

_____

_____

_____

_____

_____

_____

__Discuss your thoughts or questions about this chapter with your facilitator.__
__Have them check your work and sign here before starting the next chapter.__

Facilitator's Signature: _____

Zombie Ants

HOW DOES ADDICTION AFFECT OUR BODIES?

We've all watched or learned something that we later wish we hadn't. That happened to me while watching a nature channel show (that I can't even recall the name of now). But the topic was burned into my brain—zombie parasites. It was an entire show about parasites that use mind control, forcing their hosts to keep them alive.

The most memorable parasite from that show was one that infected ants in the rainforest. It was a fungus whose spores would burrow through the ant's skin and begin to grow in its brain. It literally turned the ant into a zombie— ordering it where to go. The confused ant would climb higher and higher before clamping onto a plant, unable to move, while the fungus killed it.

The fungus fed off the ant and then sprouted from its head, releasing spores that would fall onto the forest floor, infecting more of the ant's friends. It was disturbing and fascinating. I couldn't stop watching.

After watching that show, I haven't been able to talk about the physical effects of addiction without thinking about parasites. Addiction is a PARASITE. It feeds off its host, causing extensive damage. At the same time, it convinces us that these harmful behaviors are fun or even necessary.

Addiction makes us feel like zombies who have no choice, but that's not true. Our choices (free will) are what make us different from the ants on that show.

We aren't helpless against this parasite. Once we are aware of its presence, we can do something about it. We have choices.

In fact, exposure is deadly to parasites. If their host is aware of its presence, they can get treatment to kill it. I'm sure that if someone informed you that you had a parasite in your body, it would make your skin crawl. You'd go to a doctor to get it out. It would repulse you.

That's what we will do with addiction today. We will not allow ourselves to be fooled by the physical workings of this parasite. We will expose its destructive nature, and turn to the Lord for healing, help, and restoration.

# FINDING MEANING

As we study the physical effects of addiction, some of this may be new to you. Other parts may be a refresher of what you already know or have experienced. What's important is that we gain a clear picture of the overall physical effects of addiction.

Side Note: *Keep in mind that this is an overview of the most common physical effects. Different addictions can have different effects. Also, people can experience different effects from the same addiction. Because of this, you may experience some things that aren't mentioned today.*

What's the point of talking about this stuff? It won't change anything.

Remember what we said about what makes addiction thrive (grow)? Darkness. If we want to shine a light on addiction, we can't hide our heads in the sands of denial. We have to talk about it.

You are right though. Understanding the effects of addiction won't change them. But it can inspire us to protect ourselves from ongoing physical harm. It can also alert us to physical issues that should be examined by a doctor. And understanding enables us to bring our needs to the great physician (God) in prayer. Ignoring the physical effects of addiction does none of this.

Can't God just heal us if we put faith in Him?

God can and does. He heals many from the physical effects of addiction in a moment. In fact, if you were a long-time drug or alcohol user and didn't experience any withdrawal symptoms, God may have already done a miracle in you. Others experience healing over time. And some struggle with ongoing physical effects for the rest of their lives.

Why? This seems unfair.

While we can't answer for God, we know that He does everything for our good. God knows what we need. Some may need a miraculous healing to keep them alive or build their faith. Others may learn to rely on God by walking through the physical effects/consequences.

Whatever your path, know that your eternal salvation and healing are ensured the moment you put your faith in Jesus. Your path may be different, but you are equally saved, redeemed, restored, and loved. Don't let physical frustrations turn into spiritual doubt. Continue to trust in God.

✓ LET'S CHECK-IN

1. Those who are in the grips of addiction often stop noticing or caring about the physical damage it is doing to them. Has this been your experience or have you seen this happen in others? Please describe that here.

   _____

   _____

   _____

2. Why doesn't God heal everyone right away? What is your opinion on this?

_____

_____

_____

TALK IT OUT

If addiction acts like a parasite, then it has four survival instincts:

#1 FOCUS	#2 FUEL/FOOD	#3 GROWTH	#4 DEFENSE
Distracts & steals our focus, making it our priority—we begin to neglect ourselves.	Does damage as it feeds off us.	Uses tolerance to convince us to feed it more (increasing addictive behaviors).	Uses withdrawal to convince us to defend it and fear its loss.

> *How does addiction affect our focus?*

SHIFTING OUR FOCUS

Addictive substances or behaviors shift our focus by flooding our bodies with good feelings and/or blocking pain. How? They trigger the release of NEUROTRANSMITTERS (NTM'S) in the parts of our brains that make up the reward pathway (pleasure center). NTM's are chemical substances that influence how we feel and what we remember. They also affect our impulses to act in certain ways.

God created NTM's with purpose—for our good. They are released into the reward pathway when we interact with others, eat food, or have sex (to name a few). Their release triggers feelings of pleasure or happiness. If we follow God's standards, these positive feelings encourage survival, healthy living, and healthy relationships. The parasite of addiction hijacks what is intended for our good. It uses this reward system to push us towards harmful activities by releasing abnormal amounts of NTM's when we do addictive behaviors.

Side Note: *This is true of all addictive behaviors. Pornography, gambling, video games, and internet/ social media use all release an NTM called dopamine. Also, some drugs will block NTM's from being recycled—keeping them working longer.*

To put it simply, the NTM's released during addictive behaviors tell our brains: *you feel good, so you should remember and keep doing this activity*. This begins to shift our FOCUS, TIME, AND RESOURCES from our own growth to its growth. We begin to neglect ourselves and our most basic, physical needs go unmet, including:

➤ HYGIENE/SELF-CARE: basic self-care can become neglected (brushing teeth/hair, showers, appointments, sleep, etc.)

➤ RESOURCES: job loss (financial) and failing/dropping out of school (educational) are common

➤ NUTRITION/FOOD: malnutrition and/or severe weight loss or gain

➤ SHELTER/CLOTHING: homelessness & poverty can also occur from the loss of resources

> How does addiction feed off us?

CONSUMING ENERGY & FUEL

The highs of addictive behaviors take ENERGY which takes a toll on our bodies. Some behaviors take a larger toll on our self-care (as mentioned above), others have more severe physical consequences. In both cases, we become the FUEL/FOOD—much like those zombie ants climbing to their doom.

Addictions hijack our reward pathways (brains), giving temporary highs that mask physical damage. Here are some common examples of physical problems addictions can cause:

- Pornography abuse can cause loss of sex drive, desire, and function (Erectile Dysfunction in men).
- Alcohol abuse damages the liver.
- Smoking any drug damages the lungs.
- Stimulants can cause heart and lung damage.
- Any drug or alcohol abuse can damage the kidneys.
- Brain damage is also common among drug & alcohol users.
- Long-term damage to major organs or an overdose can lead to death.

Some of this damage can be improved (or at least limited) by stopping addictive behaviors. Some may require medical treatment. Other damage can be permanent unless healed by God. But all can be brought to Him through prayer. God is our healer.

Side Note: *Moving forward, you should get a thorough physical exam from a doctor and make regular (yearly) appointments. Inform your doctor of any history of addiction, substance(s) abused (if any), and any physical problems/symptoms you are experiencing. If drug/alcohol abuse was an issue, ask your doctor to add a note to your file stating that addictive medications should be avoided.*

> How does addiction grow?

BUILDING TOLERANCE

The parasite of addiction is never satisfied. It wants to GROW. It grows by building TOLERANCE. But what is tolerance? Remember those neurotransmitters (NTM's) we talked about? Well, the brain doesn't appreciate being hijacked. When those extra NTM's flood into it, the brain knows something is wrong and defends itself. It blocks/decreases the NTM's effects. This requires us to INCREASE the amount, frequency, or intensity of our addictive behaviors to receive the same high.

For Example: *It may take only two or three drinks for a new drinker to feel buzzed, but an alcoholic might drink two fifths before they feel anything. That is tolerance.*

Side Note: *Tolerance is built in all addictive behaviors. Gamblers take increasingly larger risks and drug users increase their dosages and frequency of use. Even pornography users escalate to more frequent, deviant, or violent materials.*

But what makes tolerance most effective is that the brain can't tell if NTM's are from normal, good behaviors or addictive behaviors. So, it blocks them all...everything becomes less pleasurable. The simple, pure joys of life become dull. Addiction grows by sucking the life out of life. The good news is that the brain can recover if we stop addictive behaviors and give it the time it needs to heal.

> How does addiction defend itself?

THE DEFENSE OF WITHDRAWAL

The best defense is a good offense. When threatened, the parasite of addiction attacks with WITHDRAWAL. Withdrawal is the negative effects we feel if we STOP addictive behaviors. Our bodies become dependent on addictive behaviors so when we stop...it reacts. This can include mental, emotional, and physical effects, but we'll focus on the physical effects today.

Some common physical withdrawal symptoms are: headaches, dizziness, sweating, chills, tingling, chest tightness and/or difficulty breathing, racing heart rates or palpitations, high blood pressure, fever, nausea, diarrhea, vomiting, stomach aches, muscle tension, sleepiness, extreme hunger, joint pain, insomnia, twitching, shakes, tremors, and more.

Alcohol and tranquilizer withdrawal can be the most dangerous and also lead to seizures, strokes, heart attacks, hallucinations, or extreme states of confusion (Delirium Tremens).

The physical symptoms of withdrawal are worse during the first few weeks of detox, but its length varies from person to person. These symptoms can create fear or an aversion to stopping addictive behaviors. We become tempted to use this as an excuse. We think, *sobriety feels horrible, so I'll keep using.*

Our enemy (satan) will use withdrawal to weave deceptions (lies), as well. His message: *You physically need this. You can't handle sobriety—you're too weak.* But these are LIES—a smokescreen. The symptoms of withdrawal are the desperate efforts of a dying parasite—addiction. Don't let it back in.

LET THE PARASITE DIE!

Side Note: *If you are going through withdrawal, remember that you are not alone. Reach out and talk to someone who has been where you are and ask for prayer and support. Also, make sure you speak up and seek medical help if your withdrawal symptoms become severe.*

✓ LET'S CHECK-IN

1. How does comparing addiction to a parasite affect how you think about it?

    _____

    _____

    _____

2. Have any behaviors or substances taken over your focus or the focus of someone you know? How has that affected you or them physically?

    _____

    _____

    _____

3. Have you or someone you know experienced tolerance or withdrawal? Describe how it affected you or them.

    _____

    _____

    _____

📖 SEARCHING SCRIPTURE

> *How can we kill this parasite and overcome the physical effects of addiction?*

▶ FIX YOUR EYES ON JESUS—YOU ARE NOT ALONE!

Let's Read: **1 Peter 4:1-5** (NIV)

This reminds us that Christ _____ in his body, and that whoever suffers in the body is done with _____.

We are NOT ALONE in our suffering. Christ suffered and died for our freedom. If you are battling symptoms of withdrawal or are frustrated with the physical effects of past addictions, fix your eyes on Jesus. Remember His pain…His suffering…His commitment. It was all for you. The physical effects of withdrawal are temporary and a small price to pay to put sin and addiction to death. Lay your pain, fear, and struggles at the foot of the cross through prayer. He understands your pain.

▶ FOCUS ON WHAT IS UNSEEN—INTERNAL & ETERNAL HEALING

Let's Read: **2 Corinthians 4:16-18** (NIV)

This encourages us to not lose _____. It reminds us that even if we are outwardly wasting away, _____ we are being renewed day by day. These troubles are

_____ and momentary. They are achieving for us an _____ glory that outweighs them all.

Again, we are reminded that these physical troubles are temporary. Remember that God is doing an internal work in us, even when we can't feel it. Our temporary struggles are setting up eternal benefits. Fix your eyes on eternal truths by reading God's Word (the Bible) and focusing on His promises.

FIND YOUR STRENGTH IN GOD

Let's Read: **Isaiah 40:28-31** (NIV)

This passage tells us that God gives _____ to the weary and increases the

_____ of the weak. Those who hope in the Lord will renew their _____.

Pray and ask God to strengthen and heal you. If you are going through withdrawal, you need His strength. Place your hope in God. His strength never fails. God will often send other people to strengthen and support you along the way too. Accept the help.

WHAT HAVE WE LEARNED? ────────────────

> Our Question: How does addiction affect our bodies?

Addiction is a _____. It feeds off its host, causing extensive damage.

The four survival instincts of addiction are:

1. _____: distracts and causes us to neglect ourselves—making it our priority

2. _____/_____: does damage as it feeds off us

3. _____: get us to feed it more by building tolerance

4. _____: uses withdrawal to get us to defend it and fear its loss

Addiction uses our own brains (reward pathways) to convince us to shift our _____,

_____, and _____ from our own growth to its growth.

The highs of addictive behaviors require _____ which takes a toll on our bodies;

Tolerance requires us to _____ addictive behaviors to receive the same high.

When threatened, the parasite of addiction attacks with _____, which is the

negative effects we experience if we _____ addictive behaviors.

You can overcome the physical effects of addiction by:

#1 Fixing your eyes on _____

#2 Focusing on what is _____

#3 Finding your _____ in God

ACTION PLAN

1 Understanding that addiction acts like a parasite isn't enough. We must get rid of it. This means creating an environment where it can't survive. The first step is obvious, stop feeding it. Stop any addictive behaviors.

List any things in your life that are feeding addiction and take steps to rid yourself of them. Bring these before the Lord in prayer and ask for His help in staying away from these things.

_____

_____

_____

_____

2 The next step is to shift your focus. Write out your thoughts or a prayer about the physical effects of addiction. Do you need healing? Do you need hope? Do you need to work on self-care and your health? Invite God into this process.

_____

_____

_____

_____

3 Now think about two simple steps you can take today or this week to take better care of your self physically (i.e. more sleep, better nutrition, exercise, focusing on hygiene, etc.).

List them here:

_____

_____

Discuss your thoughts or questions about this chapter with your facilitator. Have them check your work and sign here before starting the next chapter.

Facilitator's Signature: _____

Functional Slavery

HOW DOES ADDICTION AFFECT OUR THINKING?

I was born drunk. My mother was drunk throughout her pregnancy and my delivery. Two days after birth I went through withdrawal symptoms so severe that my doctor told my mother to put a tablespoon of whiskey in my bottle (which she continued until I was two years old).

And it never ended for me. I grabbed mom's drinks as a toddler and began sneaking alcohol into school by the age of eight. Throughout high school, I drank a fifth a day. Sadly, alcohol might have been the only consistent thing throughout my abusive childhood.

When I left high school, I graduated to two fifth's a day. And it was smooth sailing. I married a wonderful woman, joined the Navy, and had kids. I received meritorious advancements from E1 to a E5 in one year. I was excelling.

Until the day that I looked through the rear-view mirror and saw a clear reflection of myself. My mother had driven drunk often, resulting in five accidents with me in the car. One even ejected me from the car.

I swore that would never be me. It was the line I would never cross, but I just had. My children were strapped in with a drunk in the driver's seat... something in me snapped. The blinders were off. I was despicable.

When my wife called with a flat tire, I just loaded up the kids and drove. I crossed that line without a second thought. I was no longer in control. I never had been.

Every success, every promotion, was all to hide the truth, because *if there wasn't a problem, there wasn't a problem.* That's what my family taught me—a lie.

My mind and my identity had been hijacked. I could no longer trust my own thoughts. I was a slave to alcohol. My brain told me that if I stopped drinking I would die, and I let that fear and anxiety run me. It dictated my thoughts, my actions, and my emotions. Everything I did, the life I had built was to cover this ugly truth.

I was a slave...a functional slave, but a slave all the same.

~Mark's Story

FINDING MEANING

This true story shows how deceptive addiction can be. Some individuals never experience the physical effects of addiction. Mark didn't even experience physical withdrawal when he detoxed. And, socially, he experienced a lot of success.

But addiction broke him down mentally and emotionally. It was destroying him and his family from the inside out. Outwardly, he had it together. Inwardly, he hated himself. His life's foundation was a lie, and it was crumbling. He was a functional slave to alcohol (able to function on some levels but not all).

Everyone does stupid stuff when they're high/drunk. It seems like he was in control most of the time. He had his life together.

Can you hear the lie inside that statement? He was drunk—all the time. Therefore, he was never in control. He performed and got things done but that was all for show. He wanted to convince everyone that he didn't have a problem. Everything, even his success, was about supporting his addiction.

Mark knew he had a problem in high school. He tried to quit several times. He even went down to the altar for prayer at various churches, but he'd be drinking two hours later. He felt worthless. He gave up trying, and instead, worked to hide it all behind achievements. He gave up control.

Mark was mentally and emotionally enslaved. Addiction was a part of his life from birth. He didn't know what it was like to be free or to feel like he had a choice. His addiction was deeply rooted in how he thought, and he let it define him. It ruled over him. This brings us to the main point we want to explore today…

ADDICTION IS A DICTATOR!

Now I'm visualizing a short man in a suit yelling orders. How does this relate to addiction?

Well, today, we are going to talk about the mental effects of addiction. We compare addiction to a dictator because it tries to control our thoughts and choices. It doesn't want to be AN option, it wants you to think it's the ONLY option.

I think it's time that we expose how this dictator works and call it what it is—a liar. Dictators come to power by offering SIMPLE SOLUTIONS to complex problems and by LEVERAGING (USING) FEAR. Once they come to power, they make choices that benefit themselves at your expense. Why? Because their concern is power, not your well-being. Their message:

I CAN FIX EVERYTHING, JUST GIVE ME CONTROL. IF YOU DON'T CHOOSE ME, EVERYTHING WILL FALL APART—I'M YOUR ONLY OPTION.

Does this sound familiar? Addiction works in the same way. It becomes the easy solution to any problem and tells you that quitting is impossible and/or dangerous. But the truth is, addiction is the greater danger. It can be easy to let addiction take control, but the cost is your freedom. Let's begin to break these chains and renew our minds with God's truth today!

> *Isn't turning to God just exchanging one dictator for another? Doesn't He want to tell me what to do?*

Some people do view God in this way. They see Him as an angry, controlling figure who wants to take away their freedom. But I want you to think about a couple of things first.

DICTATOR	GOD
» Needs others to give them power.	» The creator of the universe doesn't need anything from you. He is all-powerful.
» Cares more about power than you.	» Sent His only Son to die for you. God is love.
» Tells you what to do to maintain control.	» Sustains the universe. Gives instructions that benefit you, and lets you choose.
» Restricts your freedoms.	» Offers you eternal life—freedom from sin, pain and death

Addiction isn't a god. It wants to be, but it isn't. Addiction and dictators are appealing because they are counterfeits to something we do need—a relationship with God. In the end, counterfeits don't hold any real value and dictators steal our freedom. God wants to free us from this worthless dictatorship.

✓ LET'S CHECK-IN

1. Have you (or someone you've known) been in denial about having addictive behaviors under control? What happened as a result?

   _____

   _____

   _____

2. What untrue thoughts or fears have made you (or someone you've known) feel trapped in an addiction?

   _____

   _____

   _____

> *How does addiction affect us mentally?*

REPROGRAMMED FOR SLAVERY

Let's Read: **Hosea 4:11 & Romans 6:6-7** (NIV)

In Hosea we see that sinful, addictive behaviors (sexual immorality & drunkenness) can take away our

_____.

Romans teaches that before we put our faith in Christ, sin rules our bodies and makes us

_____ to sin.

Life-controlling, destructive addictions affect our ability to think clearly. They TAKE AWAY OUR UNDERSTANDING. Like any successful dictator, addiction hides the truth. It confuses and manipulates our thoughts to maintain power. Its goal is to REPROGRAM our thinking so that we accept its orders.

And by doing so, we begin to think like slaves. Addictive thoughts and behaviors become normal (our default) and we become dependent. Slavery begins to sound like a good idea—*why would we want it any other way?*

Let's Read: **Exodus 14:12 & Exodus 16:3** (NIV)

In these verses we see the Israelites complaining and wishing they could return to _____.

Why is this important? Because the Israelites were slaves in Egypt for over four hundred years. God did miracle after miracle to bring them out of slavery (plagues, parting the red sea, and leading them with a pillar of cloud and fire). Despite all of that, their default when things got tough was to return to slavery.

Addiction to sinful behaviors can have this same effect. When things get tough (or even just boring), our default thinking can be: *I should just use or do xyz again.* We view our past through rose-colored glasses, forgetting the destruction, harm, and chaos those behaviors caused.

For Example: *Some prison inmates fear release because they don't know how to function outside of the system. Imprisonment feels safer than freedom—it's what they know. This thinking causes them to self-sabotage, committing crimes to extend their sentences. They choose to stay in darkness, fearing what the light might expose.*

TALK IT OUT

> *How does this work? Why do we start to think that way?*

Because addictive behaviors affect our brains. Remember those neurotransmitters (NTM's) we talked about yesterday? Well, they affect our MEMORY and our ability to think CLEARLY.

When we engage in addictive behaviors our brains are flooded with NTM's. These give us synthetic (unnatural) feelings and thoughts. We can't think clearly and our choices often suffer for it (i.e. drunk driving, inappropriate behaviors, crime, harming others, etc.). This is the immediate, mental impact.

There is also an on-going impact. Drug/alcohol abuse can lead to physical brain damage—affecting our ability to think long-term. Some of this is repairable if we stop using, but some damage can be permanent unless God heals it.

NTM's also tell us what to remember. So, the memory of our addictive behaviors gets labeled as: *a good choice*. We remember what led up to that moment and what surrounded us at the time. It's like our brains take a short video of those moments and write us a note: *remember to do this again in the morning.*

Can you see why certain places, people, smells, items, or locations can trigger thoughts about addictive behaviors? Our brains become REPROGRAMMED to seek out those behaviors or substances when they experience those cues. This reprogramming can also cause mental pre-occupation, obsession, and ritualization (patterns of thinking around addictive behaviors).

> *This stuff is a little heavy. What's the short version?*

To sum it up, addictions REPROGRAM OUR BRAINS. If you are struggling to manage your thoughts, you are not alone. If you just entered a program, you might be struggling with temptations to use or to leave. My advice: DON'T GO BACK TO EGYPT!

Slavery is not freedom, and addiction steals your future. Remember that you still have a choice. You can say NO to those thoughts. You can overthrow the dictator of addiction. Show bravery and step into freedom today—no matter what the light exposes. God stands ready to offer you a solution to these mental struggles. But first...

LET'S CHECK-IN

1. How has addiction affected you (or someone you've known) mentally?

   _____

   _____

   _____

2. Can you relate to the Israelites or the inmates we mentioned? Does what you've *known* (addiction or sinful habits) make freedom seem overwhelming or intimidating?

_____

_____

_____

SEARCHING SCRIPTURE ──────────────

> *How can we escape this dictator and get out of mental slavery?*

If you've followed the steps from our last two days (putting your faith in Christ and seeking God's healing, restoration, and strength), the next step is to allow Him to RENEW YOUR MIND. Sometimes God jump-starts this process by taking away addictive thoughts/desires all at once, and other times it's a process (like with Mark).

Either way, it is the life-long journey of any follower of Jesus for God to renew our minds from the effects of sin—becoming more like Him. Let's look to God's Word to see how this works.

PEACE OVER PANIC

Let's Read: **Philippians 4:6-8** (NIV)

Philippians instructs us to not be _____ about anything, but to let our requests be known to God through _____ and supplication (humble requests) with thanksgiving. And the peace of God will _____ our hearts and minds. We are then instructed to set our minds on whatever is _____, noble, right, pure, lovely, admirable, excellent, or praiseworthy.

DON'T PANIC – If you are battling temptation and obsessive, untrue thoughts, you might feel like panicking or bolting. You might be beating yourself up and thinking, *Why can't I get myself under control? What's wrong with me?* The more you tell yourself to stop, the worse it gets. Sound familiar?

The dictator (addiction) is desperate and trying to regain control…don't fall for it. The only power addiction holds is what you hand over to it. Don't give away your freedom by making drastic decisions or panicking.

Instead, acknowledge that you're having these fears, thoughts, or temptations. Expose them as untrue and harmful. And, (are you ready for this?) embrace peace in the middle of chaos. Philippians tells us: don't be anxious…PRAY. Bring all your fears, doubts, or obsessive thoughts to God in prayer. Ask Him to help you think clearly, thank Him for listening and caring, and wait on His peace to come.

Whether you experience an immediate release or not, keep bringing it all to God. Each time you resist temptation and choose to pray, you acknowledge God's power instead of handing over power to that addiction. You begin to transform—renewing your mind!

→ TURN YOUR THOUGHTS – turn from addictive (or sinful) thoughts to what is true, good, and pure. Even if you can only hold on to one truth right now—hold tight. In difficult times, I love to read scriptures that remind me of what is true: that I am made in the image of God (Gen. 1:27), I am a new creation in Christ - washed and purified (2 Cor. 5:17), and that God calls me His daughter (John 1:12). Find some scriptures that are meaningful to you and find rest and peace in those truths.

RENEWING AND TESTING

Let's Read: **Romans 12:1-2** (NIV)

Romans says that we should seek to be transformed by the _____ of our minds, so that by _____ we can discern (understand) the will of God (what is good, acceptable, and perfect).

→ RENEW YOUR MIND – These scriptures encourage us to offer ourselves as living sacrifices to God, turning from the pattern of this world (sin). If we turn away from sin, God will renew our minds.

We can invest in this process by reading the Bible. God's Word fills our minds with truth, replacing and combating destructive thoughts/beliefs. We can also pray and worship (spend time in His presence). As we grow closer to God, His Holy Spirit renews our minds and that addictive programming gets wiped clean.

→ TEST & DISCERN – This renewal allows us to test and discern what is true, right, and pure again. Our minds are given freedom from the dictator of addiction, but this isn't always easy—it needs testing. If you've recently stopped acting on an addiction or entered a program, your thoughts may still be confused or influenced by that addiction. It's wise to question and test your thinking right now.

Find trustworthy mentors who understand where you are to help you test your thoughts and choices. Ask them: *Does this make sense to you? Am I thinking clearly? Is this a wise decision?* This may feel embarrassing at first, but it's wise to get a second or third opinion, even about small things. When faced with a decision: pray, read God's Word, and seek wise counsel.

Side Note: *DO NOT make any drastic, extreme, or even mildly important decisions right now. Especially if you are anxious, fearful, confused, or feel pressured to act. It's better to stop, breathe, pray, and seek guidance from others.*

WHAT HAVE WE LEARNED?

> *Our Question: How does addiction affect our thinking?*

Addiction is a _____.

Addiction doesn't want to be an option, it wants you to think it is the _____ option.

Life-controlling, destructive addictions take away our _____.

Addiction's goal is to _____ our thinking so that we accept its orders.

The neurotransmitters released by addictive behaviors affect our _____ and our ability to think clearly.

Our brains become _____ to seek out addictive behaviors as a default.

Four steps to renewing our minds through Christ are:

#1 Don't _____— pray and trust in the Lord to give you peace.

#2 Turn your _____—focus on what you know to be true—find scriptures that remind you of who you are in Christ.

#3 _____ your mind—read the Bible (God's Word), pray, and worship (spend time with God)—trust in the Holy Spirit to transform and renew your mind.

#4 Test & _____—find mentors who can help you process your thoughts and decisions to make sure you are thinking clearly.

ACTION PLAN

1 If you have any unwanted thoughts or fears, write out a prayer to the Lord asking for His help, guidance, and peace. Let Him know what you are struggling with.

_____

_____

_____

_____

_____

_____

_____

_____

2 Who can you talk to about these thoughts or fears today? _____
Ask that person to help you find a few scriptures that combat these thoughts or fears. Write them here:

_____

_____

_____

_____

_____

_____

_____

_____

_____

_____

_____

_____

_____

_____

_____

_____

_____

_____

_____

_____

_____

_____

_____

_____

_____

_____

Discuss your thoughts or questions about this chapter with your facilitator. Have them check your work and sign here before starting the next chapter.

Facilitator's Signature: _____

Delayed Puberty

WHY DOES SOBRIETY FEEL SO DIFFICULT?

I was gripping an emotional live wire. Every emotion was amplified. What would be a two (on a scale of one to ten) for most people was an eight or nine for me. Simple frustrations became show stoppers—turning into anger or rage.

Anxiety and fear were intense and constant. I couldn't trust myself because I felt like sobriety would kill me. A flood of emotions were breaching the walls my addiction had built, and I couldn't cope. In fact, I had never learned how to handle any of this. Using was always my go-to.

I feel bad—I use. I feel good—I keep using. I feel nothing—I use more. Honestly, it never felt like a choice. Using was the only possibility.

"You have a choice." That's what my ninth grade science teacher told me. "You can choose to stay in my class and stop being a distraction to everyone else and learn something. Or, you can walk down to the office and be removed from my class. You have ten minutes to think about it. But decide," he said. I stood there for the full ten minutes, not thinking about his class, but about having a choice.

I had never felt that way. I was so deep into my addiction that I no longer saw anything as a choice, but it was. I didn't choose sobriety that day, but I did walk back into his class. And when I chose sobriety (six years later), he was the first person I called.

But that choice wasn't easy. Now that I was sober, I didn't know what to do. I felt lost. I felt childish. I felt dumb. I was a twenty-four year old going through EMOTIONAL PUBERTY. I couldn't handle my feelings because I had never grown up emotionally. I needed others to talk me through the most basic things.

How does a sober person handle being cut off in a line? How do I handle criticism? How do I handle worry and anxiety? How do I handle rejection? How...how...how? I was completely dependent on others. I had to learn new options.

I was completely stressed, anxious, fearful, and utterly frustrated, but for the first time in my life, I knew I had...A CHOICE.

~ Mark's Story Continued

Mark's experience is common. Many people struggle to manage their emotions after stopping addictive behaviors. But this looks differently for everyone. Anger, anxiety, fear, depression, or extreme restlessness are just a few feelings someone might experience. Some even mourn the loss of their addiction or feel like the world is dull or depressing when sober.

For others, negative emotions can become extreme. Even day-to-day annoyances feel bigger. People sometimes refer to this as a *flood of emotion*. As if all the emotions of past wounds or personal guilt come flooding in all at once. This can be overwhelming, and it reveals another characteristic of addiction…

ADDICTION IS A MASTER OF MANIPULATION.

It causes us to doubt our decisions to quit by manipulating our EMOTIONS. We may not THINK it's a good idea to use, but we FEEL like it's a good idea. It becomes impossible to trust our gut. What feels right is wrong, and what feels wrong is right. Sadly, many people quit programs or start using again because they think, *Sobriety doesn't feel good or right.* Or, *I can't handle all these emotions.*

And these thoughts are understandable as the emotions of withdrawal are often intense. But again, the only power they hold is what we give them. If we panic and make extreme decisions (i.e. leaving a program) based on those gut feelings, we can quickly find ourselves back in slavery to that addiction.

But if we choose to trust in God and acknowledge that these feelings will pass with time, He teaches us to manage these emotions. God begins to heal our wounds and He empowers us to overcome this manipulation. Addiction makes you feel like you only have one option—no choice. But the truth is that we always have a choice. In fact, there are endless combinations of healthy choices we can make in any given moment.

If Mark had been a Christian, wouldn't God have taken away those emotions?

Well, Mark was a follower of Jesus at that time and still is to this day. He testifies openly about the power of God to draw us to repentance and into freedom from addiction. But his path was not easy. He struggled with his thoughts and emotions after walking away from alcohol.

He also didn't understand why God allowed him to struggle. He became frustrated and blamed himself. He wondered if something was wrong with him or if God was rejecting him. But he overcame these doubts by trusting in the Lord.

Slowly, but surely, he began to feel better as time passed. He learned new skills and became better equipped to handle his emotions. He also learned to depend on God and others through that process. In the end, that struggle made him stronger. It taught him lessons that he has shared with countless others as an Substance Abuse Counselor today.

Some put their faith in Jesus, pray, and are immediately healed from the effects of their old addictions. Others struggle through those emotions. Whatever your path turns out to be, know that Jesus is ready and willing to walk through it with you.

✓ LET'S CHECK-IN

1. How has addiction affected or manipulated the emotions of you or someone you know?

   _____

   _____

   _____

2. Why do you think addictions affect our emotions so much?

   _____

   _____

   _____

💬 TALK IT OUT

> *Why does addiction affect our emotions so strongly?*

There are three primary ways addiction manipulates (or affects) our emotions.

#1 CREATING EMOTIONAL VIRTUAL REALITY

Once again, those neurotransmitters (NTM's) are involved. When they are released into our brain's reward pathway, they make us feel…REWARDED. We experience an emotional reward or high. And that doesn't sound so bad, except that our reward pathway has been hijacked. It's designed to reward us when we do healthy or life-sustaining things. Instead, addictions manipulate our emotions and encourage us to continue activities that damage and tear apart our lives.

For Example: *If you have experienced a trauma or are in an abusive situation, an addictive behavior might make you feel better temporarily. But that trauma still happened, and you might still be in an abusive situation. Until you work through your emotions and take steps to find safety, you are still in danger. In fact, addiction increases the level of danger and the likelihood of ongoing trauma.*

Addictive behaviors put us into a state of EMOTIONAL VIRTUAL REALITY. Virtual reality games require us to put on glasses that immerse us in a virtual (fake) world, blocking out reality. Addiction works in the same way, blinding us to the truth by making us feel good when our instinct should be to run, find safety, or make changes. When you stop your addictive behaviors (take the glasses off), painful emotions from trauma, guilt, or grief can flood back in. Going from 10 mph to 100 mph (emotionally) can be overwhelming. This brings us to our second point…

#2 STUNTING OUR DEVELOPMENT

The emotional virtual reality of addiction keeps us stuck exactly where we were when we put those glasses (addictions) on. We may think we've been moving forward, running a marathon, or whatever addiction(s) make us feel, but the reality is—we're stuck. We haven't dealt with the reality of our lives, we haven't grown, and we haven't developed the skills to cope with the challenges of life.

Our emotional development is STUNTED. So, when those emotions come flooding back in, we struggle. Just like Mark, we feel like we are going through emotional puberty. Our emotions are out of whack and we don't know how to manage them properly. We need God and others to help us learn these skills.

For Example: *An addiction to pornography might give you temporary feelings of euphoria, connection, or self-esteem, but you haven't truly connected or learned how to interact with an actual person. In fact, you learn to devalue, dehumanize, or degrade those around you. You become less equipped to develop meaningful, healthy, and God-honoring relationships.*

Side Note: *If you are in a program or newly sober, confronting the reality of where you are emotionally can be frustrating or even embarrassing. Do not let pride push you away from the help you need. You are not alone and admitting you need help is not weakness, it's wisdom!*

#3 ADDICTIONS TO CHAOS

Another issue we need to address is that we often become addicted to the chaos of addiction. Addiction often creates on-going drama and struggle. We manipulate, lie, and hussle to enable our addictive behaviors—constantly having to feed that addiction(s). We become adrenaline addicts.

When you stop the hustle, the peace of sobriety can make your skin crawl. What do you do now? What is life like when you stop manipulating and lying? What do you do when the adrenaline is gone?

If this is you, YOU ARE NOT ALONE. Let yourself breathe. If you are in withdrawal, you may also be dealing with the dulling effects of the tolerance you built. Remember how our brains defend themselves? They make NTM's less effective. The simple pleasures of life begin to feel dull, sucking the life out of life. This can lead to feelings of depression.

Emotionally, you might have gone from 100 mph to 10 mph. Understanding why this is happening can help you cope with these drastic changes. It also helps to remember that your brain will start to heal and react to the simple pleasures of life again, but it may take time. There is hope and healing is possible!

Side Note: *You may feel tempted to make extreme decisions to fill that adrenaline void. Step back and evaluate what you should be doing.* DO NOT MAKE BIG LIFE DECISIONS RIGHT NOW. *Ask others for input and really listen. If you don't, you may find yourself trading in one addiction for another.*

LET'S CHECK-IN

1. How well do you currently handle your emotions? Do you consider yourself emotionally mature? Why or why not?

   _____

   _____

   _____

2. Have you or someone you've known become addicted to the emotional chaos of addiction? How has that affected you (or them)?

   _____

   _____

   _____

SEARCHING SCRIPTURE

> *Are we just stuck feeling horrible then?*

TRADE IN THE COUNTERFEIT FOR THE GENUINE

Let's Read: **Ephesians 5:18-20 & Galatians 5:22-23** (NIV)

Ephesians tells us to stop addictive behaviors (drunkenness & debauchery) and, instead, be filled with the _____. This includes the acts of praise, worship, and declaring thankfulness to God.

Galatians lists out the fruit (results) of God's Spirit in us: love, _____, peace, forbearance, kindness, goodness, faithfulness, gentleness, and _____-_____.

For every COUNTERFEIT, there is a GENUINE, true product. The rewards that addictions provide, pale in comparison to God's design for us. He wants you to experience TRUE LOVE, JOY, AND PEACE. If you start to feel discouraged, remember that God created your reward pathway. He wants you to experience joy and pleasure. God also calls you His son or daughter and He is a generous Father.

He wants you to let go of grief and sadness to embrace His joy. Trade in fear and anxiety for a "peace that surpasses all understanding." Walk away from loneliness and depression and fall into His great love for you. Cast off the afflictions of the flesh (sinful nature), humble yourself in prayer, worship, and thankfulness, and trust in the Holy Spirit to fill you with these genuine and true blessings.

> *What if I don't feel these blessings? What if I still struggle?*

It's easy to see blessings within Scripture and want them right now. No one wants to struggle, but there are lessons to learn in the waiting. Putting our faith in Jesus is about serving and loving Him. Are there blessings attached to that? Yes. But that can't be our primary motivation. God isn't a tool to be used or a get out of jail free card. So, instead of getting impatient or beating yourself up (if you continue to struggle with difficult emotions)...PRAY AND GET TO KNOW GOD.

PEACE THROUGH PRAYER & THANKSGIVING

Let's Read: **Philippians 4:6-7** (NIV) again

This passage tells us to not be anxious, but to bring every situation to God in _____ and petition, with _____. The peace of God will then guard our hearts and minds.

Don't lose hope if the waiting lasts longer than you would like. This scripture doesn't say, *we will never feel anxious*. In fact, it assumes we will be, but it instructs us to bring that anxiety to the Lord in PRAYER with THANKSGIVING.

Thankfulness is a theme we see throughout Scripture. Just try being entitled, bitter, or angry and thankful at the same time. It's impossible. Instead, BE THANKFUL. God doesn't owe us anything. We don't deserve love, joy, and peace; but He promises them to us anyway. Trust the giver of these gifts and wait patiently.

In the meantime, invite other believers, mentors, or pastors to help guide you through this process. When you can't trust your gut, you need the counsel and perspective of those who are further down the road. You need EXPERIENCED HELP FROM OTHERS.

WHAT HAVE WE LEARNED? ————————————

> *Our Question: Why does sobriety feel so difficult?*

Because addiction is a master of _____.

It causes us to doubt our decisions to quit because it manipulates (affects) our _____.

The three primary ways addictions manipulate or affect our emotions are:

  #1 Creating Emotional _____ Reality

  #2 Stunting our _____

  #3 Addictions to _____

For every counterfeit (addiction), there is a _____, true product.

God wants us to experience true love, _____, and peace.

He also instructs us to bring any anxiety we may have regarding how we are feeling to Him in

_____ with thanksgiving.

We are called to avoid becoming entitled, bitter, or angry by choosing to be

_____.

We should also remember to seek out experienced _____ from others.

ACTION PLAN

1 Think about how you have been feeling lately. Write about how those emotions have been affecting you. How much power are they having over your decisions? Is this too much?

_____

_____

_____

_____

2 Bring these feelings to God in prayer. Tell Him how you have been feeling and ask for His strength, wisdom, and peace. Now, write down a few things that you can be thankful for today, no matter how small they might be.

_____

_____

_____

_____

3 The next step is to find someone who is trustworthy to help you process your emotions, and make good decisions that are based on truth over temporary feelings.

This week, I can ask _____ to help me with this.

In the future, _____ might be a good person to ask as well.

❚❚ *Discuss your thoughts or questions about this chapter with your facilitator. Have them check your work and sign here before starting the next chapter.*

Facilitator's Signature: _____

DAY 6 Collateral Damage

Our Question:

HOW DOES ADDICTION AFFECT OUR RELATIONSHIPS?

When people get married, they never think, *I hope we both become addicts—that would be exciting*. And when people have kids they don't say, *I sure hope they become a successful alcoholic*. Why? Because addiction DESTROYS relationships and lives.

We could start this day with a thousand different stories about the damage addiction does to our relationships. But I think we would be kicking a dead horse. We all know that addiction can ruin marriages, create abusive homes, and cause us to harm others, commit crimes, or break the most basic levels of trust with those we love.

Addiction is never a one person show. If you are in the grips of addiction and thinking, *I'm not hurting anyone but myself*—just wait. Like it or not, everyone leaves a wake (impact) behind them in life. We affect those around us and addiction will impact those around you.

The Bible tells us that we will reap (receive) what we sow (put out) (Gal. 6:7-8). Unfortunately, it seldom ends there. Those around us also reap what we sow. If you doubt that, just watch your local news. Many people become the COLLATERAL DAMAGE of the actions or behaviors of others.

As humans, we run in packs. We live within a society and we all contribute for better or worse. You can't even buy a breakfast sandwich without the help of

hundreds of others from the farm, factory, and store making that possible. We rely on and impact others. Addiction negatively changes our social impact. Even if you completely isolated yourself in a remote cabin this would still be true. Why?

Because you are here on purpose. You were designed by God, given unique talents and abilities, and you matter. Isolating yourself from the world leaves a void. Without your sowing, less is reaped.

Now, based on your history, you may think that this is for the best—less damage done. But think about the people you could help, the family you could build, or the mission you could serve if you broke free from addiction.

Remember that spiritual battle we mentioned in the introduction? Well, it's very real and you have an enemy (satan) who doesn't want you to ask these questions. He doesn't want you to know that you are purposefully designed, loved, and valued by God. He wants you used, abused, and enslaved to addiction.

Addiction is a great tool, because it ISOLATES us. Like any skilled abuser, satan's primary goals are to control, isolate, and create dependence. If this was a checklist, addiction would check off every box. Today we are going to expose these tactics, revealing how addiction affects our relationships.

43

✓ LET'S CHECK-IN

1. Do you think that everyone has an impact on others? Why or why not?

   _____

   _____

   _____

2. What kind of an impact do you have on those around you?

   _____

   _____

   _____

💬 TALK IT OUT

> *What about the damage done to me by others? That's a big part of why I am where I am. It's not all on me.*

You may be right. Chances are good that you have experienced pain or harm because of someone else's actions or neglect. But to blame others for your actions gives them an out too. They could then blame the person who hurt them, and the blame game goes on. Or, it could stop with you. The cycle stops when you acknowledge your pain, choose forgiveness, and take ownership of your own actions and choices.

> *That's easier said than done. It's not like anyone sets out to destroy all their relationships. Why does it happen so often?*

Addiction doesn't destroy all your relationships at once. No, addiction takes CONTROL, ISOLATES, and creates DEPENDENCE—gradually. We can break it down into three general phases:

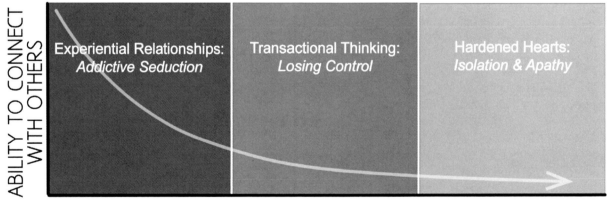

#1 EXPERIENTIAL RELATIONSHIPS - ADDICTIVE SEDUCTION

When someone begins an addictive behavior, they don't think: *I think I'll start up an addiction today.* No, it's usually more like: *That looks, sounds, or feels fun!* In fact, many start addictive behaviors out of a desire to connect with others: *Let's go out and party together! That guy/girl on the screen looks enticing. All those people in the casino look like they're having a blast!* We want to connect, and addiction seduces us with counterfeit connections.

These connections are counterfeits because they quickly become purely experiential. EXPERIENTIAL RELATIONSHIPS focus on shared experiences but lack true depth or intimacy. In these relationships, bringing up a problem or a genuine need isn't welcome—it kills the buzz (experience). The focus is always on the addictive behaviors and the answers are always—let's just do more to get your mind off it.

Side Note: *Relationships built upon addictive behaviors may feel loving/accepting. But remember that acceptance of harmful behaviors is the opposite of love. Love protects, builds up, and confronts when necessary. There is nothing loving about cheering as someone jumps off a cliff or taking them over the edge with you.*

The experiential mindset reduces your ability to connect with others as the addictive behaviors become your priority and focus. Which leads us to phase two...

#2 TRANSACTIONAL THINKING - LOSING CONTROL

As someone falls deeper into an addiction, life becomes centered on feeding those behaviors. Everything else (including other people and relationships) seem less important. We begin to think transactionally. TRANSACTIONAL THINKING means that we view and treat people as commodities (things to be used). Our relationships become a means to feed addiction(s). If people get in the way of those behaviors, they become expendable.

As this mindset grows, we start to lie, manipulate, and purposefully harm others to get what we want. We leave a trail of COLLATERAL DAMAGE (harm) in our wake. We think, *if you can't get me what I want, you're no good to me.* We dehumanize and devalue others as addiction takes CONTROL. Our relationships fall apart. This brings us to phase three...

#3 HARDENED HEARTS - ISOLATION & APATHY

Once addiction takes control, we start to lose the desire/ability to love and connect with others. We push people away and sabotage relationships before anyone gets too close. We blame others for our problems to justify our behaviors or lash out in anger if someone tries to help. We become ISOLATED and feel APATHETIC (unconcerned) about building healthy relationships.

Physical tolerance adds to this apathy because our brains become less sensitive to the NTM's naturally released when we connect with other people. Relationships don't feel as enjoyable or important anymore. We are designed to live in community, but addiction isolates us from others, creating DEPENDENCE on it. Can you see how effective this tool is for our enemy? His tactic: control, isolate, and destroy!

SEARCHING SCRIPTURE

> *After all the collateral damage, is there any hope?*

THE POWER OF CONFESSION

Let's Read: **Ezekiel 36:25-27 & 1 John 1:9** (NIV)

In Ezekiel, God has a message for the Israelites who were in exile and slavery in a foreign land.

He promises that He will cleanse them from ALL their _____ and ALL their

_____. He will give them a new _____, replacing their hearts of stone.

In 1 John, we see God's promise to us today. If we _____ our sins, God will

_____ and purify us from all unrighteousness.

Is there hope? Yes! God is in the business of taking hearts of stone and giving them NEW LIFE. But there is a catch: we need to humble ourselves and make some CONFESSIONS. Have we used, abused, and manipulated others to get what we want? Have we served an idol (addiction) instead of God? We must confess our sins, and put our faith in Jesus to forgive, heal, and restore. This is where hope is found.

Side Note: *We also have a responsibility to confess or make amends to individuals we have harmed, but we will talk more about that in PSNL 507.*

THE GOD OF RECONCILIATION

Let's Read: **2 Corinthians 5:18-20 & John 1:12** (NIV)

2 Corinthians teaches us that God _____ us to Himself through Christ and we are

given the ministry of _____.

John teaches us that all who put their faith in Jesus are given the right to become

_____ of God.

If we put our faith in Jesus, God reconciles us to Himself and then sends us out to be ministers of RECONCILIATION. Our new mission becomes about inviting others into new life in Christ—replacing hearts of stone with His loving forgiveness. God equips us to love and build genuine connections with others. Replacing the counterfeits of experiential and transactional relationships with genuine intimacy, love, and grace.

Side Note: *If you want to learn more about genuine intimacy with God and others, the Intimacy with Purpose series PSNL 105-605 is a great resource to help you grow in this area.*

And don't forget that God also calls us His SONS AND DAUGHTERS. We are no longer slaves to addiction, but members of the family of God—with an eternal inheritance of abundant, everlasting life. And this family isn't small. You are adopted alongside brothers and sisters of all races, ages, and backgrounds, who can mentor and support you along the way.

The counterfeit connections of addiction will control, isolate, and break you down. Will you allow Jesus to show you a different way? Can you humble yourself in repentance? Will you join the family of God? We are praying that you do, and we can't wait to welcome you home!

✓ LET'S CHECK-IN

1. How has addiction affected your relationships or the relationships of those around you?

   _____

   _____

   _____

2. What do you think your relationships could be like if you embraced confession and reconciliation?

   _____

   _____

   _____

WHAT HAVE WE LEARNED?

> *Our Question: How does addiction affect our relationships?*

Addiction _____ relationships and lives.

When it comes to relationships, addiction takes control, _____, and creates dependence—gradually.

The three phases of this process are:

1. _____ Relationships: based solely on shared experiences with no depth

2. _____ Thinking: treating others as commodities to be used

3. Hardened _____: isolation and apathy set in creating deeper dependence on our addictive behaviors

However, God is in the business of taking hearts of stone and giving them new _____.

To find this new life, we need to humble ourselves and make some important _____.

When we put our faith in Jesus, God calls us _____ and _____—
members of the family of God.

ACTION PLAN _____

1 We can't end this study without asking: Have you put your faith in Jesus? Are you ready to join the family of God? If you are ready, please stop right now and pray. Don't wait another moment.

It's a simple process: Just talk to God and confess that you are a sinner in need of forgiveness, that you believe that Jesus died on the cross for you to be forgiven, and that He rose from the grave to give you eternal life. Accept these gifts and invite God into your heart. Ask Him to replace your heart of stone with a heart of flesh.

2 If you prayed that prayer, take a moment to write a prayer of thankfulness to the Lord below. If you aren't ready to make that decision, write down your thoughts about it below.

_____

_____

_____

_____

_____

3 If you have already accepted Jesus into your life, what parts of your heart are still hardened towards others? Are you harboring unforgiveness, guilt about past behaviors, or apathy towards others? Write those below and then bring them to God in prayer.

_____

_____

_____

_____

_____

Discuss your thoughts or questions about this chapter with your facilitator. Have them check your work and sign here.

Facilitator's Signature: _____

WHAT DO YOU THINK?

Take a few minutes to write out (in your own words) how you would answer the following questions after completing this study.

✓ Why do we need to understand addiction?

_____

_____

_____

_____

✓ What does the Bible say about addiction?

_____

_____

_____

_____

✓ How does addiction affect our bodies?

_____

_____

_____

_____

✓ How does addiction affect our thinking?

_____

_____

_____

_____

✓ Why does sobriety feel so difficult?

_____

_____

_____

_____

✓ How does addiction affect our relationships?

_____

_____

_____

_____

Where Do We Go From Here?

When we take a step back and look at what has been exposed this week, we may be tempted to turn the light back off. We think, *can't I just un-flip that switch?* It can seem easier to accept the lies of denial, helplessness, and hopelessness than it is to face reality. But you can't un-see what we've exposed this week.

Addiction is a counterfeit, a parasite, a dictator, a master manipulator, and an isolator. It will destroy your spiritual life, wreck your body, control your thoughts and emotions, and ruin your relationships…if you let it. Let me repeat that again…IF YOU LET IT. You have a choice!

SPIRITUAL RENEWAL & ETERNAL LIFE

For every counterfeit, God has a genuine, true gift for you to embrace. Will you accept the gifts of:

THE FRUIT OF THE SPIRIT: LOVE, JOY, PEACE, PATIENCE, KINDNESS, GOODNESS, FAITHFULNESS, GENTLENESS, & SELF-CONTROL

HEALING & SELF-CARE

FREEDOM THROUGH THE RENEWING OF YOUR MIND

FORGIVENESS, RECONCILIATION & PURPOSE

No one can choose these gifts for you, and God doesn't promise this new life will be easy. But the immediate and eternal benefits are worth more than we could ever hope to give. We don't deserve and can't earn these gifts of grace, mercy, and love.

The only thing we can do is dedicate ourselves to loving God with our whole hearts, free from the idolatry of addiction. Our prayer is that you accept these gifts and allow the Holy Spirit to replace your heart of stone with a heart of flesh. Embrace God's love, face your fears, and continue to:

WALK IN THE LIGHT!

Growth Points

Take a few minutes to think about what you have learned.

Reflect

Did you complete your challenge points this week? **Yes or No**

If you did not complete them, what obstacles do you need to overcome to complete future challenge points? _____

_____

If you completed them, how did the challenge points affect you?

_____

_____

Summarize

What were the major truths (in this class) that you learned or that impacted you?

1. _____

2. _____

3. _____

4. _____

Process

How would putting these truths into practice impact your life? _____

_____

How would putting these truths into practice impact those around you? _____

_____

Action Steps

List a few steps that you can take to put these new principles into action.

1. _____

2. _____

3. _____

4. _____

Core Scripture

Review this week's Core Scripture and write it down from memory below.

_____

_____

_____

_____

_____

_____

_____

_____

_____

_____

_____

_____

Reference: _____

# Your Notes

Utilize this space to write out any thoughts, questions, prayers, or notes you may have from going through this workbook. This is also a good place to include notes from any discussions or class times you may have with your facilitator or fellow students regarding this topic.